INSTITUT DE FRANCE

Musée Jacquemart-André

Guide book

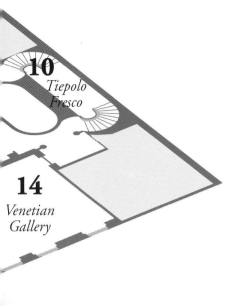

10 Tiepolo Fresco

14 Venetian Gallery

8 Winter Garden and Staircase

17 Dining Room

Introduction

The Museum façade facing the formal courtyard.

On first entering the Musée Jacquemart-André, visitors cross the threshold of the home of a pair of art collectors whose entire life was devoted to their passion for bringing together works of art. Their unique vision reflected the choices of an era, with all that means in terms of wonderment, love at first sight and artistic partiality. At all events, the collection is outstandingly innovative yet consistent - in a word, unique.

Edouard André was born in 1833 into a Protestant banking dynasty heading one of the largest fortunes of the day, which flourished at the time of the Second Empire. Inspired by Saint-Simonian and Bonapartist ideals, the family played a role in all the major ventures of the time, financed the undertakings of the incumbent regime, and helped catapult France into the modern age.

Edouard's mother died when he was two and he was reared by a stepmother who steeped him in the memory of the Napoleonic epic and prepared him for a military career. When he was eighteen, he entered the military academy of Saint Cyr, qualifying as an officer in an elite regiment in the personal service of Emperor Napoleon III.

Edouard however, preferred the glittering life at the Tuileries court, and preferred to resign his commission when the call to arms sounded. Yet he was faithful to family commitments and took over his father's seat in the National Assembly, where he represented the Gard *département*, a bastion of Protestantism.

Shortly after this, he decided to settle in the then new neighbourhood of the Plaine Monceau, where all the Imperial "gentry" had set up house, alongside the Rothschild and Pereire banking families and the Princess *Mathilde*. He commissioned the architect Henri Parent to build him a mansion worthy of the greatest in the land. The construction was inspired by 18ᵗʰ century civil architecture, but differs from it in its unprecedented sense of pomp and theatricality. The façade facing the boulevard is set back on a raised terrace, and visitors enter along a driveway that passes beneath the house, rising into a formal courtyard at the rear of the building. Inside, the majority of the space was devoted to formal reception areas whose shape

The Museum façade facing the Boulevard.

could be modified by mobile partitions to accommodate different numbers of guests. The owner's and architect's taste for theatricality are given free rein in the Winter Garden and Great Staircase - the ultimate, masterly touch in the mansion's decoration - which are placed at one end of the formal apartments.

The mansion's official inauguration in 1875 was a major event. Guests discovered the twin flights of the great staircase and its improbable equilibrium, as well as the rich materials used in the decoration. They acclaimed this achievement just as they had acclaimed the foyer of the new opera house built by Charles Garnier. The inaugural reception, which was effusively covered in the columns of *l'Illustration*, should have been followed by others, but the political climate in France and a number of Edouard's personal decisions stood in the way of this.

The Franco-Prussian war and the defeat of Sedan brought the Empire down. In 1871, the patriotic Edouard remained in Paris, where he enlisted in the *Garde Nationale* to defend the capital. When the armistice was signed, it was he who, alongside the Rothschilds, negotiated the levy to be paid to Bismarck, helping to raise the prodigious sum in a very short time.

Disappointed by the disunity reigning among the conservative political parties, he retired from public life to devote his energies to the fine arts.

1872 was thus a decisive year. He purchased the *Gazette des Beaux Arts*, and became Chairman of the *Union Centrale des Arts Décoratifs*. Master of his time, endowed with virtually limitless means, and with a house that was waiting to be fitted out, he embarked on a new venture, intending to use his mansion to revive the pomp and circumstance of the eighteenth century, a period that at the time was quite out of fashion. Yet the fact that the century of Watteau was already represented in his home did not mean that Edouard André wanted to create a conventional art gallery. Instead, he adopted the more original point of view of the *Union Centrale*, which consisted in collecting all aspects of the fine arts and combining

The Great Staircase.

5

The Grand Salon.

The Smoking Room,
ca. 1913.

The Venetian Gallery,
ca. 1913.

paintings with sculpture, furniture and *objets d'art* in a close-knit harmony.

Having been brought up to appreciate fine things, and surrounded by connoisseurs, Edouard André played all the right cards. His failing health did however stop him from coping with the demands of a project that was to occupy him for a decade, as he fitted out and decorated each room in his mansion in turn. In 1881, he married a young painter, Nélie Jacquemart, who had executed a portrait of him in 1872. Her support was to prove decisive, as she was completely in agreement with her husband's projects and had a sure touch for the siting of their acquisitions. A specific décor was chosen for each room in the mansion, to form a series of "period" rooms. Devoted to the work of eighteenth century artists and craftsmen - the painters, sculptors, cabinetmakers, and decorators who flourished in the century of Louis XV and Louis XVI - the rooms present a complete panorama of a golden age in art.

Gradually, the role played by Nélie became essential, and it was she who furnished the upper floor, which had remained empty. By way of a wedding present, Edouard gave her the central room on the upper floor which he secretly had transformed into a studio for her. But she refused to use them as such, seeing them as a space where she and her husband could exhibit the Italian Renaissance artworks they acquired on their regular forays to Italy. As they consulted with curators from all over the world, they decided to specialise in the fifteenth century and its primitive artists, which were just then being re-discovered. Every year, hundreds of artworks were transported to Paris and deposited at their home.

Simply purchasing works of art was not enough, however. They also tried to conceive a worthy exhibition space. It would take them about a decade to choose the finest of their acquisitions and bring their grand project to fruition. From 1892 onwards, they began organising their

View from the Grand Salon towards the private apartments.

The Great Staircase.

"Italian Museum", and when Edouard died, two years later, Nélie completed what they had begun together. In this way, two picture galleries and a sculpture gallery gradually brought together a selection of the most outstanding artefacts Italy had produced. The Venetian paintings that were so dear to Edouard were hung first, followed by a series of panels from Florence. Finally, the multifarious inventions of the sculptors were placed, from bronze plaques to monumental works, forming a symphony in stone without its equal.

At the turn of this century, everything was finally ready. All that remained was to refurbish the private apartments that until then had been neglected. With everything in place, Nélie set about finalising the legacy. She bequeathed the mansion and its contents to the Institut de France, on condition it used them to found a public museum. This happened in 1913. Faithful to this wish, today's display reflects the arrangement decided by Edouard and Nélie, forming a fitting tribute to their love of art, which involves presenting their residence just as much as their museum.

Nicolas Sainte Fare Garnot

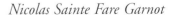

7

The Vestibule

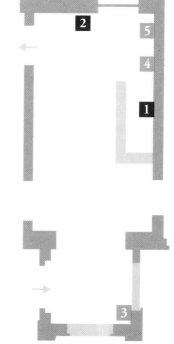

1 Gobelins tapestry factory,
tapestry from the *New Indies* series, based on designs by
Alexandre François Desportes (1661-1743)
Wool, 18ᵗʰ century.

2 Franz-Xavier Winterhalter (1805-1873)
*Portrait of Edouard André in the uniform
of the Guides de la Garde Impériale.*

3 Jean-Baptiste Pigalle (1714-1785)
Woman extracting a thorn from her foot, marble.

4 Augustin Pajou (1730-1809)
Bust of a Woman, terracotta.

5 Display cabinet, containing a green
and white Limoges biscuit-ware
dinner service by Lerosey,
11 rue de la Paix, Paris, decorated
with Edouard André's monogram.

Jean-Baptiste Pigalle (1714-1785)
Woman extracting a thorn from her foot, marble.

After climbing the steps, the visitor comes into a relatively small hall to the right of the entrance, which leads into the formal apartments, enabling visitors to proceed smoothly into the various reception rooms.

Over to the other side, a similar room precedes the private apartments originally used by the owners. Private and public spaces are thus judiciously separated. To underline this difference, the formal vestibule is nobly decorated with the discreet elegance of ionic pilasters and imitation marble stucco.

The room contains a large mirror before which Edouard André's guests would no doubt arrange themselves before greeting him. Today, visitors are met by a large, three-quarter-length portrait of the host dressed in the dazzling uniform of the Guides de la Garde. It was executed during the period when Edouard frequented the imperial couple and the Tuileries court. In accordance with his wishes, it has been placed in the hall as a way of welcoming visitors to the museum. A tapestry from the set of the New Indies woven at the Gobelins factory to a design by François Desportes serves as an ideal introduction to the mansion's decor, which mainly comprises artworks from the 18ᵗʰ century.

Gobelins tapestry factory,
tapestry from the *New Indies* series,
based on designs by Alexandre François Desportes.
Wool, 18ᵗʰ century.

Franz-Xavier
Winterhalter
(1805-1873)
*Portrait of
Edouard André
in the uniform of
the Guides de la
Garde Impériale.*

9

1 *The Picture Gallery*

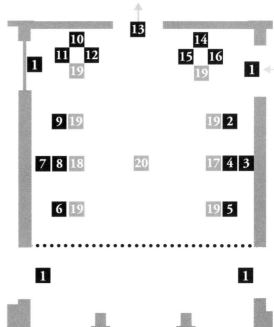

The Picture Gallery is in fact an antechamber leading into the *Grand Salon*. Externally lit by three large windows, the Gallery is designed to lead the visitor gradually into the formal apartments. It contains paintings by leading 18th century artists, hence the name of Picture Gallery.

From one wall to another the eye discovers the display scheme of Edouard André and his wife, which alternates decorative works and overdoor pieces with mythological subjects, still-lives, landscapes and portraits, fitting together like some dazzling mosaic.

There is the frivolous and sensual century of Boucher, with *Venus Asleep* and *Venus at her Toilet* ; the delicate touch of Nattier, who for once has abandoned courtly pomp to depict the features of an adolescent girl; the solid craft of Roslin or, at the other extreme, the mannerism of Drouais' *Boy playing with a cat*, one of Edouard's earliest acquisitions. In addition, there are

François Boucher (1703-1770)
*Venus adorning herself
with the attributes of Juno.*

11

François Boucher (1703-1770)
Venus asleep.

Jean-Marc Nattier (1685-1756)
*Portrait of Mathilde de Canisy,
Marquise d'Antin.*
Oil on canvas, 118 x 96 cm

*No doubt Nattier's name is not the
first to spring to mind in connection
with art in the time of Louis XV, yet
it would be difficult not to see this
painting as one of the most
outstanding in the collection. At first
sight, nothing might seem more
fastidious than this type of portrait,
but the sitter's tender years and
fragile insouciance seem to have
inspired the painter and imbued the
work with an unrivalled grace.*

Canaletto (1697-1768)
The Rialto Bridge.

Francois-Hubert Drouais (1727-1775)
Boy playing with a cat.

Canaletto (1697-1768)
Piazza San Marco.

Jean-Baptiste Oudry (1686-1755) *Heron attacked by a poodle.*

two magnificent still-lives by Chardin, the *Attributes of the Arts* and the *Attributes of the Sciences*, and two views of Venice by Canaletto which serve to remind visitors of the owners' love of this school.

After this, the eye is free to rove over the tapestry-covered benches and stools, and a collection of *objets d'art*, terracotta figures and Sèvres vases, finally coming to rest on a small polished marble statue of a *Girl with Doves*, once attributed to Jean-Baptiste Pigalle, and now set in the centre of the room to enable visitors to examine it at their leisure.

The furnishing and decoration of this ante-room reflect the ambitions of the collector. The way the works are hung means that the mobile partitions, which were designed for use during the owner's society receptions, cannot be moved. Their hanging is thus more the outcome of a museological vision. More than that, despite his love of the decorative arts, Edouard André has preferred to hang paintings guaranteed to strike the intellect. The quality of the works in their ensemble could only impress visitors. It was not until he had all the elements in his possession, during the 1890s, that he created this decor, as he sought to present it in its most complete form. Such an approach demonstrates his intelligence and sensitivity, because, more than anything else, the works assembled here are the reflection of a lifelong aesthetic rather than the fruit of some abstract science of decoration.

Jean-Baptiste Chardin (1699-1779) *Attributes of the sciences.*

Jean-Baptiste Chardin (1699-1779)
Attributes of the arts.
Oil on canvas, 140 x 215 cm

The painter of still-lives, skilled in capturing the touch of fabrics, the glint of copper or the density of matter is well known. It seems odd that this is the same artist, deftly handling a historical subject, painting objects for their allegorical value and using fabrics as the main decorative element. But this is exactly what Chardin achieves here, proving that his creative gifts were not bound by the contours of a minor genre.

13

2 The Grand Salon

1 French School, 19th century.
Four painted piers, after Watteau.

2 Gobelins tapestry set.
The Four Seasons,
18th century.

3 Chinese porcelain vases
decorated with figures.
Ch'ien period, 18th century.

4 Attributed to Jean-Baptise Huet (1745-1811)
Double gilded leather folding screen
decorated with arabesques, 18th century.

5 Jean-Baptiste Lemoyne (1704-1778)
Bust of Chancellor Maupéou, marble.

6 Barthélémy Tremblay (1568-1629)
Bust of Henri IV, bronze.

7 Carved giltwood panel covered with a tapestry
from the Savonnerie factory, depicting *Pulchinello
and Harlequin,* signed "D.P. Bertrand du Pont
à la Savonnerie" (1687-1716), Régence period.

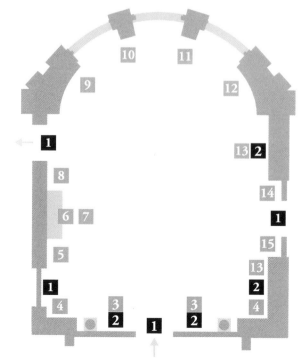

Antoine Houdon (1741-1828)
*Bust of Antoine Louis François
Le Fèvre de Caumartin,* marble.

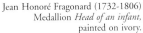

Jean Honoré Fragonard (1732-1806)
Medallion *Head of an infant,*
painted on ivory.

Jean-Baptiste Lemoyne (1704-1778)
Bust of Chancellor Maupéou,
marble.

The central *Grand Salon* of the formal apartments differs from the other rooms by its semi-circular shape, a reminder of the 18th century preference for the curve over straight lines or right angles.

It was here that Edouard André would receive his guests. During his more important receptions, he was able to fold away the lateral partitions using a system of hydraulic jacks to transform the Picture Gallery, the *Grand Salon* and the Music Room into a single area able to accommodate an even greater number of guests.

To compensate for the size of the central space, a series of half-columns have been placed around the edge of the room and on the mantelpiece. The busts placed on these comprise a sculpture gallery in their own right, an ingenious setting offering visitors a panorama of 17th century art. A number of famous figures are recognisable, including statesmen (Henri IV, Chancellor Maupéou, the Marquis de Marigny, Prince Repnine or Le Fèvre de Caumartin, a Paris magistrate), as well as famous artists (the architects Jacques Gabriel, father and son and Nicolas Vleugels, the head of the French Academy in Rome), all executed by talented sculptors such as Coysevox, Lemoyne, Houdon and Michel-Ange Slodtz.

And although the monumental dominates here, two display cases containing a collection of miniatures as well as a folding gilded leather screen attributed to Huet underscore Edouard André's fondness for the decorative arts and small collector's items. His curiosity ranged freely over the entire field of artistic creation.

15

Attributed to Jean-Baptise Huet
(1745-1811)
Double gilded leather screen
decorated with arabesques,
18th century.

3 *The Tapestry Room*

1 French School, 19th Century, overdoor decoration depicting *The Four Elements*.

2 Beauvais tapestry factory,
Tapestries from the *Russian Games* series,
emblazoned with the arms of France and Navarre,
based on designs by Jean-Baptiste Leprince
(1734-1781).

3 Francesco Guardi (1712-1793)
Venetian Portico.

4 Louis XVI commode veneered with bird's eye mahogany
and decorated with gilt bronze mounts and a slate-
blue marble top, attributed to Jean-Henri Riesner
(1734-1806), a master craftsman in Paris in 1768.

5 Louis XVI low chair in carved, giltwood,
upholstered with Beauvais tapestry,
attributed to Georges Jacob
(1739-1814).

6 Triple folding screen, decorated with
Scenes from the Theatre, 18th century.

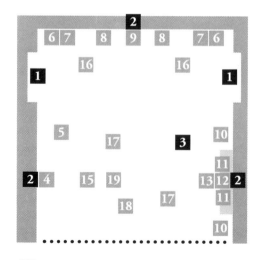

7 Pair of large Chinese porcelain jars, decorated with a *Tiger Hunt* motif, Ch'eng period (ca. 1725).

8 Pair of Louis XV carved giltwood armchairs, signed by Jacques Chenevat, a master craftsman in Paris in 1763, upholstered with a tapestry from the Beauvais factory depicting *The Fables of Jean de la Fontaine,* to designs by Jean-Baptiste Oudry (1686-1755).

9 Rosewood and kingwood *Secrétaire-cartonnier* writing desk in two parts signed by Joseph Baumhauer (Royal cabinetmaker in 1749), topped by a clock with a dial case by Charles le Roy and bronze mounts by Osmond, transitional Louis XV-Louis XVI style.

10 Pair of Louis XVI *marquises* in white painted wood outlined in gold and silver by Pierre Othon, a master craftsman in Paris in 1760.

11 Pair of Louis XVI gilt copper vases with flowers.

12 • Claude-Michel Claudion (1738-1814) *The Triumph of Galathea,* terracotta bas-relief.
• Edme Bouchardon (1698-1762) *Bust of Charles Frédéric de la Tour du Pin,* terracotta.

13 Louis XVI carved giltwood screen covered with a tapestry from the Beauvais factory depicting *Cherrypicking*.

14 Veneered rosewood and kingwood parquet regulator timepiece signed Nicolas Petit J.M.E. (1732-1791), a master craftsman in Paris in 1761. Movement signed Roggen, transitional Louis XV-Louis XVI period.

15 Carved and parcet-gilded Louis XVI basket settee, signed Pierre Othon, a master craftsman in Paris in 1760.

16 Pair of Regency cressets in carved giltwood, decorated with grotesque masks in the Boulle style.

17 Two Regency stools in carved giltwood, upholstered in petitpoint.

18 X-shaped Louis XIV stool in carved giltwood. Cushion upholstered with a fleur-de-lis tapestry from the Savonnerie factory.

19 Wool Savonnerie carpet with a pattern of foliage, dated 1663.

White marble Louis XVI fireplace from the Hotel Titon du Tillet, rue de Montreuil, Paris.

Painted ceiling : French school, 19ᵗʰ century, *Venus and Vulcan.*

Louis XVI chest of drawers veneered with bird's eye mahogany, decorated with gilt bronze mounts and a slate-blue marble top, attributed to Jean-Henri Riesner (1734-1806), a master craftsman in Paris in 1768.

Running off along the mansion's left wing is a series of more informal rooms used by Edouard André and his wife for their private and business dealings.

Situated before their study, the first of these rooms, is quite naturally an anteroom. It is special in that it was built to match the size of the three tapestries from the series of *Russian Games*, which were purchased from the dealer Mannheim in 1868, well before the house was built. The decision to display them in this way is entirely justified by their outstanding quality. They reflect the taste for orientalism that blossomed in the 18ᵗʰ century, and demonstrate the skill of the tapestry weavers at the Beauvais factory, while pointing to the importance of royal commissions.

Beauvais tapestry factory. Tapestries from the *Russian Games* series, emblazoned with the arms of France and Navarre, based on designs by Jean-Baptiste Leprince (1734-1781).

Francesco Guardi (1712-1793) *Venetian portico.*

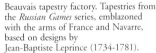

Edme Bouchardon (1698-1762) *Bust of Charles Frédéric de la Tour du Pin,* terracotta.

The tapestries also provide an opportunity to stress a further aspect of the mansion's decor, based in this case on the association of textiles and furnishings. Although not as well known as the museum's painting and sculpture collections, the furnishings and textiles are no less remarkable. The chest of drawers by Riesener, the writing desk by Joseph, and the settee and marquise armchairs by Othon all form a unified Louis XVI ensemble. Setting them off is the Savonnerie carpet dated 1663, on which is placed an easel bearing the room's only painting, a gouache by the Venetian artist, Francesco Guardi.

4 The Study

1 Attributed to Robert Levrac Tournières (1667-1752)
Portrait of a Man.

2 Jean-François Lagrénée (1724-1805)
Allegory of painting.

3 Jean-Honoré Fragonard (1732-1806)
The new model.

4 French school, 18th century,
Portrait of a Man.

5 Jean-François Lagrénée (1724-1805)
Allegory of architecture.

6 Charles-Antoine Coypel (1694-1752)
Don Quixote served by the innkeeper's daughters.
Sketch for a tapestry design.

7 French School, 18th century,
Portrait of a Woman.

8 Jean-Baptiste Pater (1695-1736)
Fêtes Galantes with dancing couple.

9 Jean-Baptiste Greuze (1725-1805)
Portrait of the engraver Georges Wille.

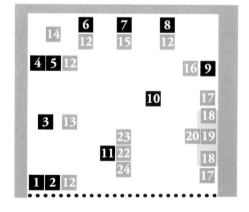

10 Jean-Baptiste Chardin (1699-1779)
Still-life with a rack of lamb.

11 Ernest Hébert (1817-1909)
Portrait of Madame Edouard André.

12 Four carved giltwood armchairs
signed Louis Charles Carpentier
(?-1787), a master craftsman in Paris in 1752,
upholstered with tapestries from the Beauvais factory
decorated with pastoral scenes.
Transitional Louis XV-Louis XVI period.

13 • Chinese lacquer fall-front secretaire, decorated with chased
and gilt bronze mounts and a white Carrara marble top,
attributed to B.V.R.B. (Bernard III Vanrisamburgh).
Transitional Louis XV-Louis XVI period.
• Phillipe Roland (1746-1816)
Bust of a Woman, terracotta.

14 • Louis XV corner cupboard in Vernis Martin with a black
marble top, signed Louis Fourreau, a master craftsman in
Paris in 1755.
• French school, 18th century,
Bust of a Man, terracotta.

15 Louis XV veneered rosewood and violet wood commode
decorated with gilt bronze mounts and a top in Breccia
marble from Aleppo. Attributed to Joseph Baumhauer
(King's cabinetmaker in 1749).

16 • Secretaire-medal cabinet in mahogany veneer with tinted
rosette marquetry and a pink Brocatello marble top
signed Pierre Denisot (1715-1782), a master craftsman
in Paris in 1746. Transitional Louis XV-Louis XVI period.
• Louis-Claude Vassé (1716-1772),
Bust of a Woman, marble.

17 Pair of Chinese porcelain vases decorated with figures in
western dress. Ch'ien Lung period (1736-1796).

18 Pair of covered Chinese porcelain jars
with green decor set
in gilded bronze.

19 Jean-Baptiste Lemoyne (1704-1778)
Bust of the Princesse de Polignac.

20 Carved giltwood fire screen decorated with a tapestry
showing *Apollo playing the lyre,* 18th century.

21 Etienne Maurice Falconnet (1716-1791)
The glory of Catherine II of Russia, marble.

22 Louis XV *bureau plat* in veneered rosewood and kingwood,
decorated with chased, gilt bronze mounts.

23 Louis XV cane-seat office chair in carved giltwood
signed Meunier,
a master craftsman in Paris, 1739.

24 19th century carpet by Braquenié
after a model from the Savonnerie
tapestry factory.

Fireplace with carved giltwood mirror frame
from the Hotel Samuel Bernard, rue du Bac, Paris.

Painted ceiling : Giambattista Tiepolo (1690-1770)
The Triumph of Hercules.

I t was here that, first Edouard André and then Nélie Jacquemart organised their day-to-day existence and their business dealings. Curiously, the room is not structured on the austere lines of a Minister's cabinet. Quite the contrary, it offers an intimate décor made up of Edouard's favourite objects.

Jean-Baptiste Greuze
(1725-1805)
*Portrait
of the engraver
Georges Wille.*

Hanging on the walls are a series of 18th century paintings, such as Fragonard's *The New Model,* a masterpiece of *libertinage.* This is framed on either side by two portraits and two allegories of the arts by Lagrénée, and a composition depicting *Don Quixote served by the innkeeper's daughters,* where the painter, Charles-Antoine Coypel, has attempted a livelier rendition than usual of a historical subject. There is also another large-scale portrait of a woman attributed to the school of Largillière, two *Fêtes Galantes* by Pater, Watteau's favourite pupil, and finally, the severe portrait

19

Louis XIV veneered rosewood and
kingwood commode with gilded
bronze mounts and a top in Breccia
marble from Aleppo.
Attributed to Joseph Baumhauer
(King's cabinetmaker in 1749).

Jean-Honoré Fragonard (1724-1806)
The new model,
oil on canvas, 50 x 63 cm.

*How to avoid licentiousness,
how to say all without telling
all, how to forget the subject
and dare set brush to canvas.
Such questions might have
been going through
Fragonard's mind as he
settled down to paint this
work. In this sketchy, sometime
careless, sometimes nervous, wor
showing brilliant spots of light as
illuminating as his brush, the
painter has fully answered his
musings, leaving the spectator astonishea
at the brilliance of it all.*

French School, 18th century.
Portrait of a Woman.

Etienne Maurice Falconnet (1716-1791).
The Glory of Catherine II of Russia, marble.

Charles-Antoine Coypel (1694-1752)
Don Quixote served by the innkeeper's daughters.
Sketch for a tapestry design.

Jean-Baptiste Lemoyne (1704-1788)
Bust of the Princesse de Polignac.

Jean-Baptiste Chardin (1699-1779)
Still life with a rack of lamb.

of the engraver Georges Wille, a work by Greuze as accomplished as it is brilliant.

When they set out to furnish the study, Edouard and his wife assembled an equally prestigious set of items, including armchairs signed by Carpentier upholstered with Beauvais tapestries, a Chinese lacquer secrétaire with bronze mounts, which could be the work of B.V.R.B., a rocaille chest of drawers with marquetry by Joseph, and a curious medal cabinet signed by Denizot, on all of which were placed a series of marble or terracotta busts. Between the two windows, a marble group by Falconnet, entitled *The Glory of Catherine II of Russia* depicts another patron of the arts in the image of Nélie Jacquemart. The centre of the study is taken up by a Louis XV writing desk with a small portrait of the lady of the house, a gift from her teacher, Ernest Hébert. The ceiling is decorated with a fresco by Giambattista Tiepolo showing *The Triumph of Hercules*, which originally graced a Venetian palace.

Throwing chronology to the winds, and with no qualms about moving from a Louis XVI room to one decorated in the style of Louis XV, Edouard and Nélie allowed themselves a few liberties with art history, because they were interested, first and foremost, in their own comfort. Here is none of the stiffness associated with the development of neo-classicism. On the contrary, the rooms are furnished with great charm and roundness, not to mention a degree of whimsicality. Unlike other areas in the mansion, they have not tried to focus exclusively on an area of artistic creation in this enfilade of rooms, seeming rather to prefer setting off a collection of artworks from a variety of disciplines. Their collectors' intuition is astounding. Recent research has brought to light the signatures of prestigious cabinetmakers on various items of furniture, which had originally escaped their vigilance.

5 The Boudoir

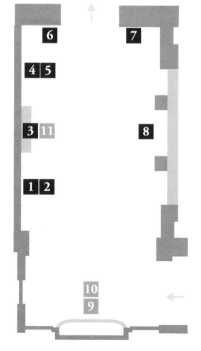

9 Louis XVI giltwood clock
with horizontal movement.

10 • Rosewood and kingwood commode
with a learned decor,
gilt chased bronze mounts
and pink Breccia marble top,
signed Pierre Roussel J.M.E. (1723-1782),
a master craftsman in Paris in 1745.
Transitional Louis XV-Louis XVI period.

• Joseph Chinard (1756-1813)
Terracotta *Bust of a Woman*, thought to be
Théroigne de Méricourt.

11 Louis XVI silk-covered
carved giltwood screen.

Louis XVI white marble fireplace
with gilt bronze mounts
and painted wood mirror frame
from the Hotel Samuel Bernard, rue du Bac, Paris.

Louis XVI mantelpiece set comprising an ornamental
clock and two gilt bronze candelabra.

Louis XVI carved giltwood chairs designed by
Georges Jacob (1739-1814), a master craftsman in 1765.

Painted ceiling : Giambattista Tiepolo (1696-1770)
Allegory of Justice and Peace.

Alexandre Roslin (1718-1793) *Self portrait.*

The wing that turns at right angles towards the boulevard comprises two bedrooms which were originally intended as Nélie Jacquemart's private apartment. Edouard had asked his architect to fit it out during their honeymoon, as a surprise for his bride.

He chose the so-called "Louis XVI-Impératrice" style for the bathroom - the style chosen by Napoleon III's consort Eugénie de Montijo, to decorate the Tuileries Palace. Like the other rooms in the mansion, however, he chose a mix of ancient and modern, installing a marble fireplace from the Hotel Samuel Bernard and ordering new panelling from elite craftsmen.

Louis XVI giltwood clock
with horizontal movement.

Joseph Chinard
(1756-1813)
Terracotta *Bust of a Woman*,
thought to be Théroigne de
Méricourt.

Rosewood and kingwood
commode with a learned
decor, gilt chased bronze
mounts and pink Breccia
marble top,
signed Pierre Roussel J.M.E.
(1723-1782), a master
craftsman in Paris in 1745.
Transitional Louis XV-Louis
XVI period.

When it was remodelled in the 1890s, the first of the two rooms retained the original alcove, the site of the bathtub, with its balustrade surmounted by a large mirror. There are doubts as to whether it was later used as an oratory or a small music room, and its original use was forgotten until it was rediscovered during a search in the archives. Today the bathtub has been replaced by a commode by Roussel, with a terracotta bust by Chinard sometimes identified as the heroine of the French Revolution, Théroigne de Méricourt. The rest of the room is furnished with a neo-classical ensemble of gilded Louis XVI furniture and old masters. Associated with the type of portrait that his wife so loved, this ensemble of neo-classical

Jacques-Louis David (1748-1825)
*Portrait of Count Antoine Français
de Nantes, State Counsellor,*
oil on wood, 114 x 75 cm.

*The main efforts of the painter David went
into this kind of heroic realism, of which
this is a masterly example. It is said that he
borrowed the costumes of his sitters so that
he could take his desire for verisimilitude to
the extreme. But he also handles his subjects
like antique marble effigies. In the final
analysis, what he gives us is the ideal image
of the great civil servant, with all that
implies in terms of authority and severity.*

24

Francois Taurel (1757-1832)
View of a French port.

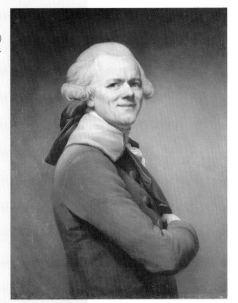

Joseph Ducreux (1735-1802)
Self portrait.

Pierre-Paul Prud'hon
(1758-1823)
*Portrait of Charles-Louis
Cadet de Gassicourt.*

furnishings concludes Edouard André's excursion into his favourite century. The portrait of *Countess Skavronskaia* reminds us of the taste for the royal court, and the woman who was the favoured portraitist of Marie-Antoinette, while David's canvas of the *Comte Français de Nantes* evokes the formality of imperial etiquette. This amusing confrontation is resolved by the touch of irony in Ducreux' *Self Portrait,* while the melancholic reverie of the *Portrait of Charles-Cadet de Gassicourt,* painted by Pierre-Paul Prud'hon in Italy, serves as a prelude to Romantic sensibility.

Lastly, floating high above these works, so different in spirit yet of equal quality, Tiepolo displays his greatness in the *Allegory of Justice and Peace,* on the Boudoir ceiling, the ultimate homage to the decorative fantasies of the period.

Louise-Elisabeth
Vigée-Lebrun (1755-1842)
Portrait of Countess Skavronskaia,
oil on canvas, 135 x 95 cm.

Is there such a thing as women's painting? Although the model is graceful and suggests all that might rightly be said to belong to the so-called weaker sex, the artist endows the sitter with qualities we previously ignored in her, chooses a pose and decides on the colouring. In other words, composes a work that will transcend nature without the artifice appearing unusual. The outcome of this creative energy is a masterpiece, and it matters little whether the maker is man or woman.

25

6 The Library

1 Antony Van Dyck (1599-1641)
Portrait of a judge.

2 Attributed to Pierre Sauvage (1744-1818)
Children playing, grisaille.

3 Antony Van Dyck (1599-1641)
Time clipping Cupid's wings.

4 Frans Hals (1580-1666)
Portrait of a Man.

5 Jan de Bray (1626-1697)
Portrait of a Man.

6 Rembrandt Van Rijn (1606-1669)
Portrait of Dr Arnold Tholinx.

7 Antony Van Dyck (1599-1641)
Portrait of Count Henri de la Pena.

8 Rembrandt Van Rijn (1606-1669)
The Supper at Emmaus.

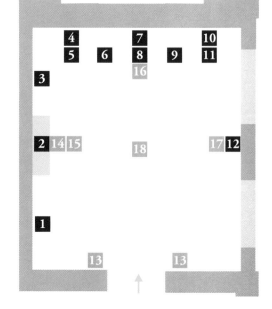

9 Rembrandt Van Rijn (1606-1669)
Portrait of Amalia van Solms.

10 Judith Leyster (ca. 1600-1660) (attrib.)
Laughing child.

11 Philippe de Champaigne (1602-1674)
Portrait of a Man.

12 Jacob Van Ruysdael (1628-1682)
Landscape near Haarlem.

13 Bronze-mounted Brazilian rosewood cupboard,
Régence period. Contains a collection of Sèvres
and Saxe biscuitware and porcelain.

14 • French school, 18th century.
  Bust of Louis XVII, marble.
  • Louis XVI burnished
  gilt bronze candelabra.

15 Régence giltwood screen
covered with a flower-vase
patterned tapestry on a white ground.

16 Marquetry cabinet with ivory inlay in a dark-stained
pearwood, forming a pattern of bouquets and birds.
Flanders, 17th century.

17 Marquetry stained wood table with an ivory inlay.
Pattern of flowers. 19th century.

18 Showcase containing a collection of Egyptian antiquities,
topped with a bronze statuette of *Moses,*
by Andrea Riccio (1470-1532).

Crystal Chandelier with chased gilt bronze.
Restoration period.

Painted ceiling : French school, second half
   of 18th century, *Minerva.*

Antony Van Dyck (1599-1641)
Time clipping Cupid's wings.

Originally Nélie Jacquemart's bedroom before it became a library, this room stands at one extremity of the mansion. It was here that Edouard and Nélie would pore over the sale catalogues and plan their future purchases. The two glass-fronted cases used to contain the antiquarian books and precious bindings that, as expert bibliophiles, they so loved. For conservation reasons, these have now been replaced with their collection of French and German Sèvres and Saxe china. Among the earliest pieces collected by Edouard André, he showed them at the exhibitions organised by the *Union Centrale des Arts Décoratifs.* The walls are hung with a series of 17th century Flemish and Dutch paintings.

Frans Hals (1580-1666)
Portrait of a Man.

27

It might seem surprising that Edouard André should break the rules he had set himself. But he knew how much the northern masters had influenced the French artists of the following century, and was aware of the link some claimed with their artistic forebears. It was perfectly normal, therefore, that he should show interest in these old masters and that he should seek to bring together some fine examples.

Rembrandt Van Rijn (1606-1669)
The Supper at Emmaus.
Oil on Canvas, 39 x 42 cm.

During his lengthy career, Rembrandt painted the theme of the Pilgrims at Emmaus on a number of occasions. There is no doubt that the Musée Jacquemart-André version is the most striking and the most successfully executed. When the painter draws on all the resources of artificial light and plunges the scene into deep obscurity, skilfully drawing on the manner of Caravaggio, he doubtless does so in order to augment the work's dramatic intensity. And in this case, what might at first sight seem an anachronism, is transformed into a metaphysical interpretation, in the literal sense of the word, as close and as faithful as possible to the scriptures.

28

Antony Van Dyck (1599-1641)
Portrait of a judge.

Jacob Van Ruysdael (1628-1682) *Landscape near Haarlem.*

Philippe de Champaigne (1602-1674)
Portrait of a Man.

Small as it is, the collection is most eloquent. Here are a *Portrait of a Judge*, the epitome of the Flemish character, and a rare mythological subject, *Time Clipping the Cupid's wings*, both by Van Dyck. Nearby is the incredibly modern brushwork of Frans Hals' *Portrait of a Man*, rubbing shoulders with the meticulous and more traditional rendition of a Jan de Bray. And the Rembrandts! Hanging here are his *Portrait of Doctor Tholinx*, the *Supper at Emmaus*, and a profile *Portrait of Amalia van Solms*. The three works admirably span the career and stylistic development of the master. Few museums can claim to offer visitors such an outstanding itinerary, ranging from the acute, delicate realism of his early period to the surreal vision of his maturity to the dramatic tenor of the evening of his life. Elsewhere in this room, a portrait by Philippe de Champaigne reminds us of another aspect of the Flemish tradition, with its poetic realism. And how better to conclude this impressive series of masterpieces than by losing oneself in one of Ruysdael's tumultuous landscapes?

Some time later, Nélie introduced an unusual note into the library by placing an octagonal glass case in the centre of the room. This contains the collection of Egyptian antiquities she brought back from one of her long trips and which reflect her eclectic tastes.

Rembrandt Van Rijn (1606-1669)
Portrait of Dr Arnold Tholinx.

Rembrandt Van Rijn (1606-1669)
Portrait of Amalia van Solms.

29

7 The Music Room

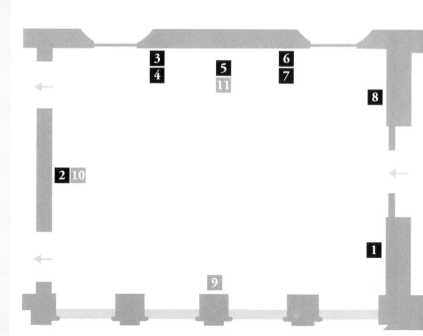

Jean-Honoré Fragonard
(1732-1806)
Head of an old man.

After retracing our steps and crossing the *Grand Salon*, we enter the Music Room in the other wing. No other room in this mansion better reflects the spirit of the Second Empire in its area and height. The architect has been inspired by formal reception rooms such as those at the Tuileries or in the Rothschild's *Chateau* at Ferrières, with their heavy décor and crimson brocade hangings.

Built on two levels, it has a painted, vaulted ceiling depicting *Apollo Protector of the Arts* by a decorator much in vogue at the time, Pierre-Victor Galland.

Edouard André's Cavaillé-Coll organ was installed on one side of the mezzanine, and it was here that the musicians would sit on concert evenings. It was here too that, towards the end of her life, Nélie Jacquemart would receive the composers of the Paris school. In her papers are letters of thanks signed by the likes of Fauré, Vincent d'Indy and Debussy.

Soothed by the strains of music that seem to descend from heaven, visitors can admire more famous works of French painting, such as Hubert Robert's *Ruined Gallery*, portraits by Perronneau, a *Head of an Old Man* by Fragonard, whose expression contrasts strongly with the elegant *Three-quarter Portrait of a Man,* which remains anonymous, despite being attributed to a variety of great artists. There is also a portrait by Largillière, and finally, an *Architectural Capriccio*, the invention of the Italian Panini, although it was long attributed to his pupil, Hubert Robert. Standing beneath a Beauvais tapestry depicting a *Banquet after the Chase* to a design by François Boucher, is a bronze bust of Edouard André at the end of his life by Nélie Jacquemart, the only bronze she ever executed.

31

Hubert Robert (1733-1808)
Ruined gallery.

1   Greco-Roman art, Hellenistic period.
Statue of wingless Victory, marble.

2   Roman art, 3rd century AD.
Sarcophagus with bas-reliefs representing
Minerva and Ceres, marble.

3   Copy after ancient Greek sculpture.
Bas-relief of *Bacchante,* plaster.

4   Greco-Roman art, 2nd century AD.
Votive stele, marble.

5   Venetian school,
first half of 16th century,
Bust of an Emperor, bronze.

6   Studio of Allessandro Vittoria (1525-1608)
Venice, 16th century,
Bust of a bearded man, marble.

7   Allessandro Vittoria (1525-1608)
Bust of the Countess Diana Tenderini, marble.

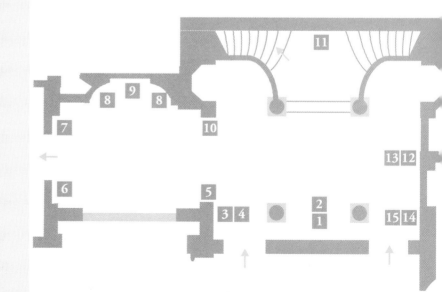

- **8** • Roman art, Imperial period.
    Wreathed, fluted column.

  • Roman art, ribbed vase with handles, marble.

  • Roman art, fountain basin, marble.

- **9** Greco-Roman art. Full-length statue of a
  Woman carrying a bunch of grapes.

- **10** Venetian school, first half of the 16th century.
  Bust of a woman, bronze and alabaster.

- **11** Jean Warin (1604-1672)
  Bust of Cardinal Richelieu, bronze.

- **12** Italian school, 16th century.
  Bust of Augustus wearing a breastplate, marble.

- **13** • Roman art, imperial period.
    Altar-shaped cippus, Carrara marble,
    Augustan period.

  • Greek art, 2nd century AD.
    Statue of *Eros,* marble.

- **14** Italian school, 16th century.
  Medallion, stone.

- **15** Greco-Roman art.
  Statue of Woman wearing a toga, marble.

Behind the Music Room is another space, the Winter Garden, which was typical of contemporary socialising, and which came into vogue during the reign of Napoleon III. The fashion developed in Britain and was very successful. The idea was to have an area roofed with glass containing mostly exotic plants. This leafy area would enable guests to rest briefly in a cooler atmosphere than in the adjacent stuffy rooms.

Jean Warin (1604-1672)
Bust of Cardinal Richelieu, bronze.

Greco-Roman art,
Hellenistic period.
Statue of wingless Victory,
marble.

The architect, Henri Parent, gracefully bowed to his patron's request that a Winter Garden be included in the overall design. Nevertheless, Parent suggested an even more lavish decor in order to make the mansion exceptional. So far, we have not seen any staircase leading to the upper floor. Usually, it would be placed in the central part of the volume or just to one side. Here, however, the architect has decided to situate it at one extremity of the building. This original choice may perhaps be explained by Parent's urge to surpass his rival, Charles Garnier. Using a bearing wall and two marble columns, Parent designed a formal staircase which, turning twice, rises directly to an elliptical cornice without recourse to an intermediate landing. The purely functional aspect of the staircase has thus been rejected in favour of a theatrical spectacle designed as a joy for the eye. Thanks to Parent's technical prowess with visual effects, his love of décor and his balanced mix of surprise and overcharged detail, we are blessed with a staircase the like of which has never been seen before or since.

33

9 The Smoking Room

1 Sir William Beechey (1753-1839)
Portrait of a young woman in a riding habit.

2 Sir Thomas Lawrence (1769-1830)
Portrait of the Duke of Buckingham.

3 English school, 18th century,
Portrait of two sisters.

4 Sir Joshua Reynolds (1723-1792)
Portrait of Captain Torryn.

5 John Hoppner (1756-1810)
Portrait of Mrs Inchbald.

6 John Hoppner (1756-1810)
Portrait of a young woman.

7 English school, 18th century,
Portrait of a woman.

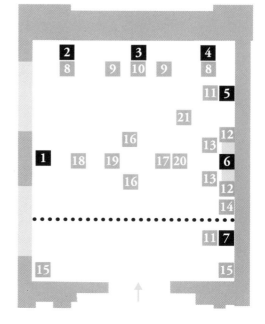

8 Pair of incense burners with flower pattern, cloisonné enamel. China 19th century.

9 Pair of terracotta dragons glazed with a black slip. China, 19th century.

10 Carved wood sideboard, French school, 15th century, fitted with a showcase containing:
 - An enamelled glass mosque lamp, Syro-Egyptian, 14th century.
 - Two bowls from the studio of Bernard Palissy (1510-1590).
 - A salt-cellar in Saint-Porchaire earthenware, France, 16th century.
 - Two enamelled earthenware plates, Persia, 14th century.
 - Two repoussé copper bowls, Persia, 14th century.

11 Carved, inlaid cabinets in tropical woods. Indo-Portuguese, 17th century.

12 Pair of vases in Imari porcelain. Japan, early 19th century.

13 Andrea Briosco ("Il Riccio"). Bronze figures.

14 Venetian ceremonial helmet, standing on a giltwood cresset, 16th century.

15 Pair of Chinese cloisonné enamel vases. Floral pattern on turquoise background, 19th century.

16 Two poufs upholstered with polychrome fabric in Arabian pattern.

17 Fourteenth century Italian octagonal carved oak table fitted with a glass case containing Islamic antiquities.

18 Persian wool carpet, Iran, 18th century.

19 Ouchak carpet, Anatolia, 16th century.

20 Ottoman carpet, wool, Egypt, 16th century.

21 Damascus carpet, Syria 16th century.

Marble fireplace emblazoned with the arms of the Micheli family of Venice. Italian school, 16th century.

Ceiling : Venetian School, 16th century.
The Quarrel between Minerva and Neptune.

Enamelled glass mosque lamp, Syrio-Egyptian, 14th century.

The final room in the series of formal apartments was mainly reserved for the gentlemen. It was to this room that they would retire after dinner to savour fine cigars and brandy.

Sir Joshua Reynolds (1723-1792)
Portrait of Captain Torryn.

Sir Thomas Lawrence (1769-1830)
Portrait of the Duke of Buckingham.

Originally, Edouard had the walls covered with imitation Cordoba leather (made from papier maché), and decorated the ceiling with a mythological scene depicting the *Quarrel between Minerva and Neptune concerning the Foundation of Athens,* executed by a pupil of Tintoretto.

After her husband's death, Nélie Jacquemart remodelled the room to suit her own more relaxed taste. During a trip to England, she purchased a series of 18th century English portraits. At a time when the leading French museums had still not recognised their talent, she was collecting works by Lawrence, Gainsborough and others. It was this same insatiable artistic curiosity that urged her on long overseas trips. As she discovered new horizons, she brought back with her a whole world of remarkable artefacts which she assembled in this smoking room, to form an arresting ensemble of *objets d'art* which includes oriental carpets, Persian antiquities and Indian furniture, under the detached gaze of a *Man Playing a Lute* by Francesco Salviati.

35

Ceiling : Venetian School :
The Quarrel between Minerva and Neptune.
16th century.

1 Giambattista Tiepolo (1696-1770)
Henri III being welcomed by the Doge Contarini, fresco.

2 Parts of three tapestries,
Flanders, 17th century.

3 Italian school, 18th century,
Statues of *Hercules* and *Diana,* marble.

4 • Late 15th century Italian wooden table.

• Italian school, 16th century.
After Benvenuto Cellini,
The rape of Ganymede, earthenware.

5 Spanish school, 17th century.
Full length *Portrait of a man.*

6 French school, 16th century.
The rewards of virtue and the dangers of pleasure,
Embroidered tapestry.

7 Venetian school, 16th century.
Portrait of Count Gambara.

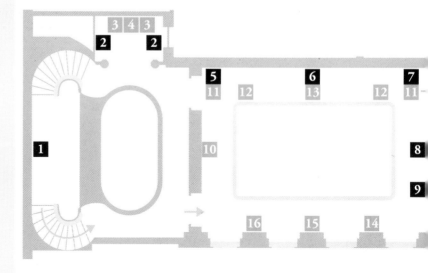

8 16th century Brussels tapestry.
Christ carrying the cross,
to a design by Barent van Orley (1488-1541).

9 Titian (ca.1485-1576).
Portrait of Hercule d'Este.

10 Gilded, carved oak sideboard fitted
with a glass case containing Italian majolica
and Venetian glass.

11 Italian 16th century
carved giltwood chests.

12 Louis XV burnished bronze mantelpiece vases
on bronze supports painted to resemble Boulle work,
decorated with Louis XIV chased,
gilt bronze mounts.

13 16th century carved giltwood
oak bench.

14 Venetian school, 16th century.
Bust of a woman, bronze.

15 Gian Lorenzo Bernini (1598-1680)
Bust of Pope Gregory XV, bronze.

16 Venetian school, 16th century.
Bust of Giangiacomo Trivulzio,
bronze.

Gian Lorenzo Bernini (1598-1680)
Bust of Pope Gregory XV, bronze.

In 1893, the illusion of the staircase was reinforced by the acquisition of a set of frescoes by Tiepolo, brought here from the Villa Contarini at Mira, near Venice. Their sheer size made this a remarkable undertaking Moreover, the location chosen to show them created a particularly strong effect of surprise. Like the figures depicted in the central panel, visitors discover the frescoes gradually as they mount the staircase. And with the page whose legs dangle outside the frame, or the lovely Venetian ladies who seem to be leaning over the balcony for a better view of the scene, visitors also discover the trompe l'oeil effect so dear to the fresco painter and the André's alike.

At the top of the staircase, visitors cross to the other side of the mezzanine to enter the *Italian Museum,* heralded by a glass case containing a selection of Italian glass. Three extremely rare bowls manufactured in the Murano workshops demonstrate the island's debt to Byzantine art. A series of enamelled china plates and dishes trace the development of ceramics from the Hispanic workshops that had inherited their skills from Persia and the Middle East, down to the creations of Gubbio, Deruta and, of course, Faenza, in what is now Italy.

A few more steps take the visitor past a series of bronze and burnished terracotta busts, among which is one of Pope Gregory XV by Bernini. Two tapestries also hang in the Musicians' Gallery, one of which is the celebrated *Christ Carrying the Cross*, woven in Brussels in the fifteenth century, and the other a curious embroidered tapestry, probably of French origin. Chief among the portraits is Titian's *Hercule d'Este.*

16th century Brussels tapestry. *Christ carrying the cross,*
to a design by Barent van Orley (1488-1541).

37

1
- Attributed to Francesco di Simone Ferruci (1437-1493)
  Virgin and Child, medallion, painted stucco.
- Attributed to Benedetto da Rovezzano (1474-1522)
  The Archangel Michael and Lucifer, marble.
- Florentine school, 15ᵗʰ Century, marble doorway.

2
- Florentine school, 15ᵗʰ century.
  Hadrian, marble.
- Tuscan school, 15ᵗʰ century, alcove, marble.
- Venetian school, 15ᵗʰ century,
  Bust of Niccolo Orsini, marble.
- Lucca school, 16ᵗʰ century, *Christ*, marble.
- Venetian school, 14ᵗʰ century.
  Virgin and Child, terracotta.

3
- Bartolomeo Bellano (1430-1496)
  Christ taken down from the cross, burnished terracotta.
- Venetian school, first quarter of the 14*th* century.
  Doorframe, Istrian stone.

4
- Florentine school, 15ᵗʰ century.
  After Antonio Rosselino, *Virgin and Child*,
  painted, gilded stucco.
- Domenico di Paris (fl. Ferrara 1450-1470)
  Virgin and Child, painted, gilded stucco.
- Florentine school, 15ᵗʰ century. After Antonio Rosselino.
  Virgin, Child and three cherubim, painted stucco.
- Gian Cristoforo Romano (ca. 1465-1512)
  Portrait of Capilliata Colleoni, marble.

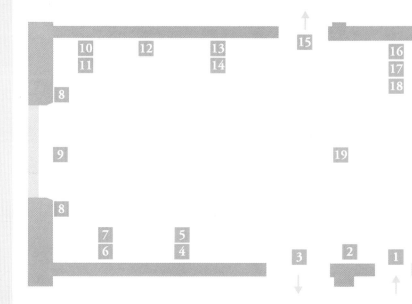

Francesco Laurana (fl. 1458-1502)
Bust of a Princess, marble.

Usually, the so-called "noble" storey of a private mansion would be taken up with the private apartments of the owners. For reasons unknown, Edouard André did not ask his architect to fit out the first floor, which stood unused until 1881, when he had the central area set up as a painter's studio for his wife. He had no compunction, at that point, about having the façade of the upper storey remodelled so that his wife could get the light from a large widow. But Nélie soon gave up her activity as a portrait painter, and used this area as a store room for her personal effects.

Some time around 1890, however, they decided to exhibit their collection of Renaissance artworks here. In this project for an *Italian Museum* they were probably following the example of their curator friends. It was at this period that the great European museums like the Bargello in Florence, the Bode Museum in Berlin and London's National Gallery were being set up. Consequently, the couple set aside a succession of three rooms for their paintings, objets d'art and sculptures.

The first of these, originally Nélie's studio, contains a rich collection of Italian sculpture. To the left on entering, visitors discover a first panel which reveals Nélie's preference

39

Donatello (1386-1466)
Pair of bronze
cherub cressets.

The Sculpture Gallery-Rotunda

1 Girolamo da Vicenze, 15ᵗʰ century.
Martyrdom of Saint Sebastian.

2 Pietro di Giovanni di Ambrogio
(fl. 1428-1448).
Saint Catherine in glory.

3 Francesco Botticini (1446-1497).
Virgin and Child between Saints John the Baptist,
Pancras, Sebastian and Peter.

4 Venetian school, 16ᵗʰ century. Monumental stone
doorway with archivolt and wooden doors.

5 Francesco Cossa (1436-1477).
Virgin and Child, stained glass.

6 • Domenico Rosselli (1439-1497).
Saint Jerome, stone.

• Domenico Rosselli (1439-1497).
Saint Aldebrand, stone.

7 Luca della Robbia (1400-1482).
Virgin and Child, white enamelled earthenware.

40

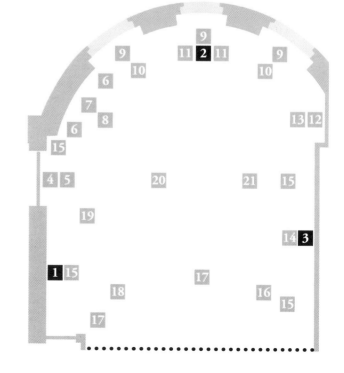

for harmony rather than historical consistency. On an inlaid chest, she has placed two *Bronze cherub cressets* by Donatello and a marble *Bust of a Princess,* attributed to Francesco Laurana. Above these, three bas-reliefs depicting the profiles of three historical characters are set into the wall. Finally, three framed stucco representations of the *Virgin and Child* are hung on the wall to offer the eye a summary of the various genres and techniques practised during the period.

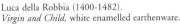

Luca della Robbia (1400-1482).
Virgin and Child, white enamelled earthenware.

Donatello (1386-1466).
*The Martydom
of Saint Sebastian,*
bronze.

Facing these, the same search for harmony dictates the way the works are organised around a monumental drinking fountain and the uprights of an elegantly carved doorframe. To the right of this, the ceiling has been deliberately lowered to form a fine, semi-circular rotunda containing examples of decorative sculpture. Among these are a series of polychrome earthenware medallions made in the workshops of the Della Robbia family. Seeking to achieve a variety of effects, Nélie has also hung three paintings in this room: a Venice school *Martyrdom of Saint Sebastian*, a banner by the Siennese painter Pietro de Ambrogio, and an altarpiece by the florentine master, Botticini, depicting the *Virgin and Child with Four Saints*.

41

The central area contains tables, polychrome or gilded statues and a glass case containing three of the most priceless pieces: a bronze plaque depicting a Saint Sebastian by Donatello, and two ewers in Medici porcelain.

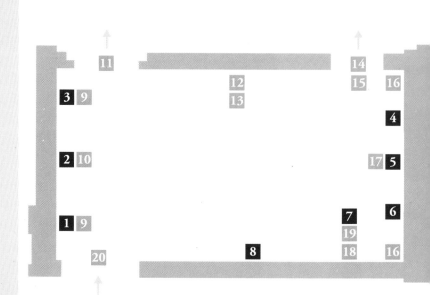

O riginally, this room contained a collection of *objets d'art*. In her letters, Nélie Jacquemart called this room a *cabinet*, in the old sense. According to these early descriptions, a collection of small objects, small-scale plaques, medals and tokens were exhibited here, as well as parchments, jewellery and ceramics illustrating the rich variety of Italian decorative arts.

Pietro Vanucci Perugino (1445-1523). *Virgin and Child.*

All this changed after the death of Edouard. Nélie had often expressed the desire to focus more on Florence than on the rest of Italy. In fact, later on, she wanted to purchase a villa in the hills overlooking that city, but was unable to find the palace of her dreams and abandoned the quest. She then decided to build a mausoleum in the form of a private chapel containing all her most precious belongings. Presented both as a place of worship containing artworks inspired by religion (eg, choirstalls, an altarpiece, a funeral monument), the room is also a picture gallery that concentrates on the Florentine school of painters. Several depictions of the *Virgin and Child* provide a variation on this theme enabling visitors to study their similarities and differences.

43

Paolo Uccello (1397-1475).
Saint George and the dragon.
Painted wood panel,
52 x 90 cm.

*Nélie Jacquemart could not have
been unmoved by the bizarre charm
of this small panel, purchased late
in life on the London art market.
Its attribution to one of the greatest
masters of the Florentine school,
who at the time was still
unrepresented in her museum,
amply justified the acquisition.
More important than this however,
is the way it hovers between a
narrative mode inherited from
medieval tradition and the new
theories of the Renaissance, of which
Uccello was one of the propagators.*

44

Alessio Baldovinetti (1422-1499).
Virgin and Child.

Francesco Botticini thus shows the vast distance separating the master from the pupil. Sandro Botticelli offers us a youthful masterpiece, while Pietro Vanucci has executed a masterly work that has been miraculously well preserved. Finally Alessio Baldovinetti demonstrates the remains of the archaic style in his depiction. On their own, these three works would suffice to place this room among the most priceless in the museum. Also hung here is one of Ucello's workings of the *Saint George and the Dragon* theme, an enigmatic work that seems to waver between two inspirational genres and two modes of expression.

Attributed to Paolo Schiavo (1397-1462).
Visit to the delivered mother.

Sandro Botticelli (1444-1510).
Virgin and Child.
Oil on wood, 62 x 48 cm.

Long attributed to the studio of Verrocchio,
which was indeed its source of inspiration,
this work was recently returned to Sandro
Botticelli. The elegance of the composition,
the juvenile grace of the child and the maternal
tenderness emanating from the Virgin Mary
all argue for this new attribution.
It is a further example of that rare quality,
possessed by both Nélie and Edouard, the
"connoisseur's eye", which enabled them to
recognise the hand of the great master among
a host of painted panels.

45

14 The Venetian Gallery

1 Andrea Mantegna (1430-1506).
Virgin and child between Saint Jerome and Saint Louis of Toulouse.

2 Attributed to Andrea Mantegna (1430-1506).
The legend of Saint Christopher, three-panel predella.

3 Andrea Mantegna (1430-1506).
Ecce Homo.

4 Carlo Crivelli (1440-1494).
Saints Louis of Toulouse, Jerome and Peter.

5 Giovanni Bellini (1430-1516).
Virgin and Child.

6 Andrea Mantegna (1430-1506).
Virgin and Child surrounded by figures.

7 Carlo Crivelli (1440-1494).
Saint Bernard, a saintly bishop and Saint Bartholomew.

8 Attributed to Domenico Morone (1432-1503).
Virgin and Child against a city background.

9 Lazzaro Bastiani (ca. 1449-1512).
Legend of an unidentified saint, three-panel predella.

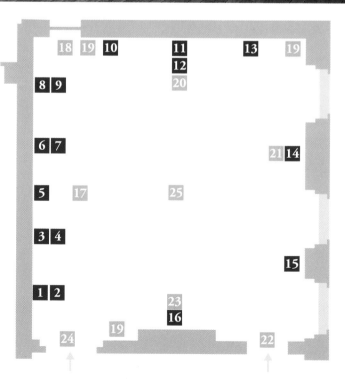

This third room of the Italian museum is perhaps the one that owes most to Edouard André's personal taste. Arranged during his lifetime, it contains a collection of fifteenth century paintings which for the most part are from Venice or its zone of influence. After his wife converted him to an appreciation of Italian Renaissance art, he developed a preference for Venetian works.

At the time, the collectors and curators who made this choice were few and far between, since Florence was all the rage. Edouard André's selection is even quite astonishing : several examples of Andrea Mantegna's work are hung here, including a poignant *Ecce Homo*. Alongside these, a *Virgin and Child* by Giovanni Bellini reminds us of the family and artistic ties uniting the two painters, while a predella by Bastiani epitomises the Venetian school's detailed, highly-coloured creations.

On the wall facing the entrance are a group of works by Crivelli, Schiavone and, most importantly, Vittore Carpaccio. These are imbued with a medieval spirit or reflect the continuing influence of Byzantine art from the preceding generation. They are strangely archaic, demonstrating the existence of an artistic direction other than that of the Tuscan humanists, one

Section of grisaille ceiling
attributed to Girolamo Mocetto
(ca. 1458-1531).

Andrea Mantegna (1430-1506).
*Virgin and Child between Saint
Jerome and Saint Louis of Toulouse.*

47

Carlo Crivelli (1440-1494).
Saint Bernard, a saintly bishop and Saint Bartholomew.

Andrea Mantegna (1430-1506).
Ecce Homo.
Oil on canvas, 54 x 42 cm.

A fervent admirer of classical art, Andrea Mantegna imbues his figures with the formal solidity of the sculptors of antiquity. Yet he never forgets to introduce a sense of humanity, making this particular image of the suffering Christ a genuinely moving experience.
The tragic premonition of the destiny to be accomplished, His total solitude and the mockery He must endure, transform this hieratic painting into a compelling, poignant drama.

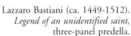

Lazzaro Bastiani (ca. 1449-1512).
Legend of an unidentified saint,
three-panel predella.

Giovanni Bellini (1430-1516).
Virgin and Child.
Oil on wood, 131 x 103 cm.

Many Italian painters have depicted the Virgin and child in interpretations as charming as they are maternal. In this particular work, we are charmed by the Virgin's majesty, seated on a royal throne, reminding us of her dignity and suggesting the divine nature of the child she is presenting. Today we are forced to see this work charged with a different meaning, to the extent that some art historians believe it to be a royal commission. It is not known exactly when it was purchased or under what title it was offered to Nélie Jacquemart and Edouard André. They selected it, however, despite its irritating anonymity, hanging it right in the centre of the wall panel, as if they had kept it the best place. The outstanding chromatism, ethereal luminosity and daring simplification of form all prompted the experts to identify it as one of Bellini's last paintings.

Cima da Conegliano (1459-1518).
Virgin and Child.

based on a brilliant association of matter and colour serving a picturesque narrative style. Additional works by Bernardo Luini and Cima de Conigliano confirm the influence of this north Italian centre.

Finally, the several items of Renaissance furniture, including a ceremonial bench bearing the arms of the Strozzi family, and above all a painted compartmented ceiling attributed to Mocetto, sound a decorative note in this exhibition room which seeks to recreate the ambience of a Venetian palace.

Vittore Carpaccio (1465-1526).
*The visit of Hippolyta, queen of the Amazons,
to Theseus, king of Athens.*
Oil on wood, 102 x145 cm.

*When he purchased this work in Austria,
Edouard André was aware that this was to be one
of his major acquisitions, since there are so few
of Carpaccio's works outside Italy. Although the
identity of the painter is beyond doubt, there
remain questions about the origin and the
significance of the subject. Should we see in it an
allusion to some political action, the signing of
a treaty, the commemoration of some diplomatic
event transformed into an allegorical narrative,
or an illustration of a successful poem which is
credited - wrongly - as being one of the founding
texts of the Renaissance? The artist has depicted
Theseus as an old man of senatorial mien, while
Hippolyte and her retinue are phoney warriors,
transforming the scene into a splendid carnival
procession where the picturesque and decorative
intention dominate.*

Vittore Crivelli (?-1502). *Saint Bonaventure.*

49

15 Nelie's Bedroom

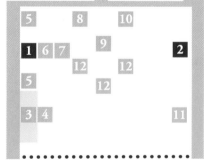

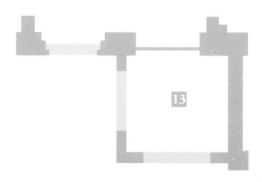

8 Veneered rosewood and kingwood oval bedside table with Aleppo Breccia marble top,
signed Dusautoy (1719-1800), J.M.E,
a master craftsman in Paris in 1779.

9 Carved giltwood bed, 19ᵗʰ century.

10 Veneered rosewood and kingwood oval bedside table with Aleppo Breccia marble top, signed Nicolas Petit, a master craftsman in Paris in 1761.

11 • Chinese lacquer panelled commode with gilt bronze mounts and Aleppo Breccia marble top signed D.F. (Desforges), a master craftsman in Paris in 1739.
• Jean-Jacques Caffieri (1725-1792).
Bust of a man, dark-burnished terracotta.
• Pair of chased gilt bronze wall light fittings, Regency and Louis XVI period.

12 Persian carpet, Turkey, 18ᵗʰ century.

13 Small sitting-room adjacent to the bedroom containing :

▪ A pair of Paris porcelain fruit baskets with Edouard André's monogram, 19ᵗʰ century.

▪ Ernest Hebert (1817-1909)
Portrait of Nélie Jacquemart.

▪ Mahogany cylinder-top bureau,
Paris workshop, 19ᵗʰ century.

▪ Nélie Jacquemart (1841-1912)
Portrait of a Girl.

▪ Two Chinese cloisonné enamel baskets,
19ᵗʰ century.

▪ Mahogany side-table with white marble top.
Paris workshop, Empire period.

▪ Pair of bergère armchairs, carved giltwood.
Paris workshop, 18ᵗʰ century.

▪ Carved, polished wood settee.
Paris workshop,
18ᵗʰ century.

▪ Louis XVI-style giltwood chair.
Paris workshop, 19ᵗʰ century.

▪ Mameluk carpet,
Turkey, 18ᵗʰ century.

▪ Engraving, *Portrait of a woman* in profile.
19th century.

▪ French school, pair of terracotta vases
to a design by Claude Michel Clodion
(1738-1814)
19th century.

When Nélie Jacquemart lived in this mansion, she was more intent on creating a showcase for the collection than on her personal comfort. It was not until the Italian Museum was finished, therefore, that she found time to renovate her private apartments.

In these, she chose to return to a Louis XVI atmosphere, as shown by her bedroom, which is an outstanding example of the genre. Around the wide bed she had specially made, she installed antique wood panelling, and brought in some of her finest items of furniture, such as the Chinese lacquer chest of drawers by Desforges and a host of the little tables with which she loved to surround herself. The walls are covered with Lyons silk, on which hang two pastels, including a *Portrait of a Man* by Maurice Quentin de la Tour, whose quality contributes to the magnificence of the décor.

Maurice Quentin de la Tour
(1704-1788)
Portrait of a man, pastel.

51

Jean-Jacques Caffieri (1725-1792).
Bust of a man,
dark-burnished terracotta.

16 The Antechamber and Edouard's Bedroom

1 Hermann Winterhalter (1808-1891).
Portrait of Ernest André.

2 Hermann Winterhalter (1808-1891).
Portrait of Madame André.

3 Nélie Jacquemart (1841-1912).
Portrait of Edouard André.

4 Hermann Winterhalter (1808-1891)
Portrait of Edouard André as a child.

5 Guillaume Coustou (1716-1777)
Pan teaching Apollo to play the flute, terracotta.

6 Carved giltwood screen covered with a tapestry showing ducks, to a design by
Jean-Baptiste Oudry (1686-1755).

7 Small Louis XVI
marquetry rosewood table.

8 Carved giltwood
Louis XV screen.

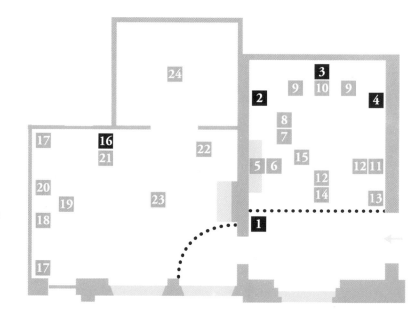

9 • Carved giltwood
   Louis XV *marquise.*
   • Louis XV *duchesse brisée,*
   carved giltwood.

10 • Louis XV marquetry commode with rosewood and
   kingwood, gilt bronze mounts and a pink Pyrenees
   marble top, signed François Garnier,
   a master craftsman in Paris in 1742.
   • Attributed to Jean-Baptiste Lemoyne (1704-1778).
   Bust of a woman, terracotta.

11 Louis XV rosewood marquetry
   dos d'âne bureau.

12 Carved, lacquered wood Louis XVI-style chairs,
   Paris workshop, 19th century.

13 Small, Louis XV sitting-room table attributed to
   B.V.R.B. (Bernard II Van Risenburgh),
   a master craftsman in Paris in 1730.

14 Oval marquetry table with floral marquetry designs,
   Paris workshop, 19th century and set
   with an 18th century Meissen tea service.

15 Louis XVI carved lacquered medallion armchair
   and footstool.

16 Attributed to Jean-Baptiste Greuze (1725-1805).
   Genre scene.

17 Louis XV carved giltwood chairs upholstered
   with Aubusson tapestrywork, signed by Tillard
   (1685-1766).

18 Directoire mahogany table
   with a white marble top.

19 Carved giltwood bed,
   Paris workshop, 19th century.

20 Louis XVI trough writing table with
   rosewood and kingwood marquetry.

21 • Veneered Louis XV coffin-shaped commode
   with gilt bronze mounts and a Poster marble top,
   attributed to B.V.R.B. (Bernard II Van
   Risenburgh), a master craftsman in Paris in 1730.
   • Jean-Baptiste Carpeaux (1827-1875).
   Bust of Edouard André, plaster.

22 Louis XVI carved giltwood *marquise*
   armchair signed J.B. Boulard (1725-1789),
   a master craftsman in Paris in 1750.

23 Louis XVI style carved giltwood *duchesse brisée.*
   Paris workshop, 19th century.

24 Bathroom :
   • Louis XVI carved, painted wood console
   with green edges, Italian workshop,
   late 18th century.
   • Louis XVI style carved, painted close-stool,
   Paris workshop, 19th century.

It is in this room and the next that the memory of Edouard is the most alive. In the antechamber, his presence is marked by a series of family portraits, including one of himself, painted by his future bride in 1872. A collection of personal effects, including his father's wallet and an engraving of all the deputies in the National Assembly during his term of office ensure that his presence lives on.

His bedroom, together with the adjacent bathroom, were refurbished after his death, which is why they are perhaps more evocative of a female presence. Placed on a transitional-period commode attributed to B.V.R.B. is a plaster bust of Edouard by Carpeaux. Despite the resemblance with the Emperor, this is definitely a portrait of the owner, and an ultimate testimony of Nélie Jacquemart's admiration for and loyalty to her husband.

Attributed to Jean-Baptiste Lemoyne
(1704-1778).
Bust of a woman, terracotta.

53

17 *The Dining Room*

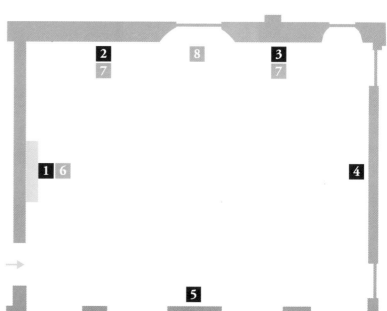

1 Workshop of Jean-François and Pierre Van der Borght, Brussels, 18th century, to a design by Jean Van Orley (1665-1735), tapestry from the Story of Achilles series : *The combat between Diomedes and Eneas, Diomedes lifts the stone.*

2 Workshop of Jean-François and Pierre Van der Borght, Brussels, 18th century, to a design by Jean Van Orley (1665-1735), tapestry from the Story of Achilles series : *The combat between Menelaus and Paris.*

3 Workshop of Jean-François and Pierre Van der Borght, Brussels, 18th century, to a design by Jean Van Orley (1665-1735), tapestry from the Story of Achilles series : *The baby Achilles is immersed in the waters of the Styx by his mother Thetis.*

4 Workshop of Jean-François and Pierre Van der Borght, Brussels, 18th century, to a design by Jean Van Orley (1665-1735), tapestry from the Story of Achilles series : *Paris elopes with Helen.*

5 Workshop of Jean-François and Pierre Van der Borght, Brussels, 18th century, to a design by Jean Van Orley (1665-1735), tapestry from the Story of Achilles series : *The combat between Diomedes and Eneas : the duel.*

6 Denis Puech (1854-1942) *Bust of Nélie Jacquemart*, marble.

7 Two carved giltwood consoles, one from the Régence period, the other 19th century.

8 • Italian school, 17th century. Group of figures and cherubs carrying a shield, forming the tympanum of a marble funeral monument.

• Pair of chased, gilt bronze wall light fittings attributed to Jean-Jacques Caffieri (1725-1792).

Painted ceiling : Giambattista Tiepolo (1690-1770). *Fame heralding the visit of King Henri III*, trompe l'œil.

Now the Museum's coffee-shop, the final room, located next to the entrance hall was, of course, originally the dining room. The sheer size of the space and the quality of the décor prove just how important the dining room was in the day-to-day life of the mansion.

Around the walls are a series of Louis XV carved giltwood consoles used as sideboards, while a bust of the mistress of the house graces the mantelpiece. Hanging on the walls, five 18th century tapestries from the Achilles series, woven in Brussels, narrate the hero's deeds during the Trojan wars. Their colours have remained remarkably fresh.

The most surprising work in this room is the ceiling painting, a work by Giambattista Tiepolo. Like the painting on the Great Staircase, it was brought here from the Villa Contarini in Mira. Despite its allegorical title of *Fame Heralding the Visit of King Henri III*, the trompe l'œil effect, the characters leaning against the balustrade and the monkey with its tail hanging over the ceiling arch communicate a somewhat comic, theatrical atmosphere. The artist seems also to have included a self-portrait, leaning over the balustrade to greet the visitor...

Tapestry from the Story of Achilles series : *The baby Achilles is immersed in the waters of the Styx by his mother Thetis.*

55

Painted ceiling by Giambattista Tiepolo (1690-1770) Detail.

The André Family

E douard André, who built up the collection of artworks described in this guide, died in 1894, two years before his cousin, Alfred André. Since both died childless, with them was extinguished a lineage whose 300-year history was marked by great events.

Portrait of Joseph André (1736-1802).

T he André family came from the Vivarais region in southern central France. The earliest trace of the family dates back to the first third of the fifteenth century. For five generations, the eldest sons were notaries both at Sanilhac, their birthplace, and at Largentière, the local capital, while the younger sons were established locally in prosperous families.

Although the advent of the silk industry passed them by, the André family, like the famous Olivier de Serres who promoted it, nevertheless rallied early to the Reformation. But the Edict of Nantes, designed to promote religious freedom and the reopening of Protestant churches fell largely on deaf ears in these distant "Marches", and the repression was as severe as the initial surge was powerful. From the end of the sixteenth century, people began returning to the fold of official religion in increasing numbers.

Perhaps it was for this reason, perhaps for reasons of individual entrepreneurship, that a younger André moved south to the city of Nîmes in 1600. The glorious ancient Roman city was at that time shaking off a bout of sleepiness that had lasted several centuries. The trade in skins and in wool was nurtured by the recent arrival of an abundant source of labour from the Cévennes mountains David-André accordingly set himself up as a wool dyer and merchant, and like most of his peers, lent money at interest.

David André's three sons were the driving force behind the rise of the dynasty. In 1647, the eldest allied himself with the opulent Privat family in Geneva, while the second remained in Nîmes. The youngest, David II, founded a trading company in Genoa in partnership with the Boissier d'Anduze family. The time was 1667, and Genoa the Superb was a flourishing city state, opposing Louis XIV's Spanish policies by protecting French Protestants. When the Edict of Nantes was revoked in 1685, the Andrés were already at the head of one of the most important Genoese merchant houses and were able not only to welcome their brothers and sisters in religion, but also, because they had emigrated some time before, to enter and leave France at will.

At this time therefore, the house of André was three-headed, with bases in Nîmes, Genoa and Geneva. The Nîmes branch was in silk and, with a couple of other families, soon controlled the entire industry, from the manufacture of the skeins of silk in the Cévennes, to the manufacture and export of finished goods (especially stockings), as far afield as Peru. The Genoese establishment, which officially became a bank in 1728, continued to deal in luxury goods, but was above all active in maritime lending and changing money, and the acceptance and discounting of bills of exchange. Geneva served as a base for an activity that was swiftly becoming international. And although it was to Geneva that the Andrés generally retired at the end of their working lives, they also contracted a number of matrimonial alliances there. With the Privat family, once again, and with the La Rives on several occasions, not forgetting the Necker circle: his brother, Necker de Germany, and then, on two occasions, with the Girardots, their allies. It was thus that the affiliates set up in London in 1748 and in Paris in 1775 became, quite naturally, correspondents or partners.

In the 1770s, Nîmes was the sixth or seventh most important city in the kingdom. Its prosperity was based on its Protestant middle class who, because civil and military careers were closed to them due to their religious persuasion, threw themselves into trade and money. The city was famous for its ancient monuments such as the Coliseum, the Maison Carrée, or the Pont du Gard aqueduct. Its *Académie* enjoyed great prestige because the membership of Jean-François Séguier, and his "universal culture" and outstanding collections attracted everybody who was anybody in Enlightenment Europe. A stop at Nîmes was *de rigueur* for anyone undertaking the Grand Tour.

Those members of the André family who had remained in Nîmes - four brothers - sold their house in the rue des Cardinaux, where they had lived since 1619, and settled in the rue Dorée. On the ground floor were the warehouses and the office of Jean, whose apartments were on the so-called "noble" floor. The urbane and refined David lived on the second floor, with Jean-Jacques, a member of the *Académie* and a friend of Séguier, in the rear wing, and Joseph the traveller in the garden apartments, when he was not in Genoa, Cadiz or Paris - where for want of time he had refused a position with the Neckers. The furniture was in the latest fashion, while Joseph's collection of paintings was unrivalled in the

whole of the Languedoc. When he moved to Paris in 1796, he took the finest with him, yet left behind in Nîmes a Titian, two Holbeins, a Correggio fresco, a Subleyras and around twenty other lesser works.

The André brothers were men of the Enlightenment, as witnessed by their library. They welcomed the French Revolution enthusiastically, while the *fêtes et académies* celebrations they threw in Genoa were rapidly transformed into a political club. An anonymous denunciation even went so far as to compare Joseph with the philosopher Jean-Jacques Rousseau ! Two years later, three of them were listed as belonging to the *Feuillants.* But they were moderates and supporters of a constitutional monarchy who were to be ruined by the Revolution. Jean, who had resigned from the Nîmes commercial court, went to the guillotine in 1794 for his Federalist beliefs. His possessions were confiscated and his establishment closed.

In Genoa in 1792, his son Dominique filled a contract to supply wheat worth more than 6 million *livres* for the French government. This was followed by two others, one for the Gard *Département*, the other for the French Army in Italy. But the young merchant had to advance enormous sums that the Directoire was unable to repay. In 1798 a ruined Dominique André sold up in Genoa and returned to Paris.

At the time, he was 32 years old, ambitious and resolute. Better still, his credit was intact. He opened a new business in the rue de Cléry and shortly after settled in the former Hotel de Ligne, rue du Mont Blanc (now the Chaussée d'Antin), the financial district of the time. He sailed untroubled through the crisis of 1815, which almost engulfed the fledgling Bank of France. Earlier,

Portrait of Ernest André (1803-1864) by Hermann Winterhalter (1808-1891).

Portrait of Madame André, Edouard's mother, by Hermann Winterhalter (1808-1891).

Portrait of Edouard André as a child by Hermann Winterhalter (1808-1891).

Portrait of Alfred André (1827-1896),
photographed by Nadar.

Edouard André's Family Tree

in 1808, he had taken on one of his nephews, François Cottier, as a partner. Thanks to their close partnership and their complementary contributions, the house of André flourished when business returned to normal after the Restoration. It took part in all the major public and private financings: Government bond issues, the creation of the National Savings Bank, the big insurance companies, canal construction and property developments in the new Poissonnière and Saint Lazare districts of Paris among them.

Dominique André retired a millionaire in 1834. Two of his sons had earlier joined him in business : Jean, the eldest, and then Ernest, who married François Cottier's daughter. Their son was Edouard André, who thus inherited the bank's fortune on both sides of the family.

The bank continued to prosper during the July Monarchy and the Second Empire, headed by Ernest André and Adolphe Marcuard, a Swiss partner. Then came the turn of Alfred André and André de Neuflize, respectively Jean André's son and son-in-law. Among other projects, they had a hand in the creation of the Paris-Orleans railway, they had business interests in the new Eldorado in the Far East, took part alongside other great merchant banks in setting up the Banque Impériale Ottomane and

in exploiting the Nile Delta, although they were not completely successful in this area.

Defeat in the Franco-Prussian war of 1870-71 and the resulting collapse of the Second Empire brought further change. Edouard André retired from public life to devote himself to his collecting, to the *Union Centrale des Arts Décoratifs* and the *Gazette des Beaux Arts.* His cousin Alfred played an active role in the Administration of the City of Paris when the Prussian armies were besieging it, and in the negotiation and payment of the reparation demanded by Bismarck in return for his restricting the time of occupation to a single symbolic day.

After briefly flirting with politics as a Deputy for Paris in the 1871 general election, Alfred then divided most of his time between his role as unchallenged head of the merchant bank and his tireless work for Protestant charities.

Thus, Edouard and Alfred each live on today in their own way, the former in the shape of the collection he bequeathed to the Institute and the latter through the families of nephews and associated friends who have kept alive the traditions which he himself did no more than pass on.

Virginie Lehideux-Vernimmen

Dominique André
Lyons 1766 - Paris 1844
x (1793)
Marie Rivet († 1857)

Marie-Jean
Genoa 1794 - Paris 1850
x (1825)
Henriette Walther († 1886)

Louis-Eugène
Paris 1800 - Paris 1861
x (1836)
Adélaïde de Neuflize († 1868)

Ernest
Paris 1803 - Paris 1864
x (1832)
Louise Cottier († 1835)

Marie-Louise
Paris 1826 - Paris 1907
x (1847)
André de Neuflize († 1868)
Neuflize line

Alfred-Louis
Paris 1827 - Paris 1896
x (1858)
Alice Joly de Bammeville
(† 1889)

Gabrielle
Paris 1838 - Paris 1907
x (1852)
Henri Mallet († 1908)
Mallet line

Georges
Paris 1846
Paris 1875

Isabelle
Paris 1836 - Paris 1869
x (1858)
Frédéric Monnier († 1894)
Monnier line

Edouard
Paris 1833 - Paris 1894
x (1881)
Nélie Jacquemart († 1912)